Parenting for Academic Success

A Curriculum for Families Learning English

Unit 8:

Playing With Language

PARENT WORKBOOK

Lesson 1: Songs and Nursery Rhymes

Lesson 2: Clapping Games and Language Play

National Center for Family Literacy

DELTA PUBLISHING COMPANY

Copyright © 2005 by the National Center for Family Literacy

Parent Workbook 8   ISBN-10: 1-932748-36-9
                      ISBN-13: 978-1-932748-36-9

Acknowledgments

Parenting for Academic Success: A Curriculum for Families Learning English was developed by the National Center for Family Literacy (NCFL) in collaboration with the Center for Applied Linguistics (CAL) and K. Lynn Savage, English as a Second Language (ESL) Teacher and Training Consultant.

Principle Curriculum Authors: Janet M. Fulton (NCFL), Laura Golden (CAL), Dr. Betty Ansin Smallwood (CAL), and K. Lynn Savage, Educational Consultant.

Special thanks to the Toyota Family Literacy Program, which piloted these materials in Washington, DC; New York, NY: Providence, RI; Chicago, IL; and Los Angeles, CA.

The Verizon Foundation provided original funding for the development of this curriculum and supports the National Center for Family Literacy in its development of resources for English language learners. Verizon's support of the literacy cause includes Thinkfinity.org, a free digital learning platform that advances learning in traditional settings and beyond the classroom. Visit the Thinkfinity Literacy Network managed by the National Center for Family Literacy and ProLiteracy Worldwide on Thinkfinity.org for free online courses and resources that support literacy across the life span.

Special thanks to Jennifer McMaster (NCFL) for her editing expertise.

A Message for Parents

This program is designed for parents who want to build their English language skills. The program also will help you learn ways to help your child improve his or her skills to succeed in school.

You will do activities to learn and practice reading, writing, speaking and listening in English. These activities also share information about how children learn to speak and read English. Each lesson has an activity you can do with your child at home.

When you support your child's learning at home, your child learns how language works.

Doing family learning activities together:

- Helps you be your child's first teacher.
- Helps you learn how your child learns.
- Makes learning fun.
- Supports your child's learning outside the classroom.

You can help your child learn every day. This program will help you help your child to learn.

Un Mensaje para Padres

Este programa está creado para padres que quieren mejorar sus destrezas en inglés. A la misma vez el programa les va a ayudar apoyar el aprendizaje de sus niños y a prepararlos para tener éxito escolar cuando entran a las escuelas.

Dentro encontrarán actividades para que mejoren sus destrezas de lectura, escritura, y conversación en inglés. Las actividades van a compartir información acerca de cómo aprenden los niños a hablar y leer en inglés. Cada lección tiene actividades para hacer en casa con sus niños.

Cuando usted apoya el aprendizaje de su niño en casa, él o ella aprende como se usa el lenguaje.

Cuando hacen actividades escolares juntos:

- Le ayuda ser el primer maestro de su niño.
- Le ayuda aprender como aprende su niño.
- Aprendiendo conceptos es más divertido.
- Apoya el aprendizaje de su niño fuera del salón de clase.

Le puede ayudar a su niño diariamente. Este programa le ayuda apoyar el aprendizaje de su niño.

LESSON 1: Songs and Nursery Rhymes

Lesson Goal
Learn and practice strategies for playing with language to support your child's language and literacy development.

Lesson Objectives
Today we will:

▶ Identify and sort words that rhyme.

▶ Identify and sort words that begin with the same sound.

▶ Substitute beginning sounds in words.

▶ Practice songs and nursery rhymes you can share with your child.

Lesson Warm–Up
1. Sing this song with your teacher and class.

The Good Morning Song

<u>Good Morning</u>

Good morning, good morning,
How are you? How are you?
Very well, I thank you.
Very well, I thank you.
How about you? How about you?

Good afternoon, good afternoon,
How are you? How are you?
Very well, I thank you.
Very well, I thank you.
How about you? How about you?

Good evening, good evening,
How are you? How are you?
Very well, I thank you.
Very well, I thank you.
How about you? How about you?

<u>Buenos Días</u>

Buenos días, buenos días
¿Cómo estás? ¿Cómo estás?
Muy bien, gracias.
Muy bien, gracias.
¿y usted? ¿y usted?

Buenas tardes, buenas tardes
¿Cómo estás? ¿Cómo estás?
Muy bien, gracias.
Muy bien, gracias.
¿y usted? ¿y usted?

Buenas noches, buenas noches
¿Cómo estás? ¿Cómo estás?
Muy bien, gracias.
Muy bien, gracias.
¿y usted? ¿y usted?

2. What songs did you sing as a child?

I sang _____.

3. Who sang with you when you were a child?

_____ sang with me when I was a child.

4. What songs do you sing with your child?

I sing _____

_____

_____.

Points to Remember

Sing songs and say nursery rhymes with your child. It will help your child:

▶ Hear and learn language sounds.

▶ Use knowledge about sounds to learn to read and write.

▶ Have fun playing with language sounds and sound patterns.

Can you add some more important points to this list?

_____

_____

_____

_____

ACTIVITY 1: Key Vocabulary

Words in this lesson are listed below. Use the Key Vocabulary pages to build your vocabulary.

1. Review the words. Which ones do you know?

Word Part	Word	Example	Translation
noun	beginning sound		
noun	ending sound		
noun	nursery rhyme		
noun	rhyme	*A rhyme is a kind of poetry.*	
noun	song		
noun	sound		
verb	listen		
verb	rhyme	*The word "ten" rhymes with "hen."*	
verb	sort		
verb	substitute		

2. Practice Key Vocabulary words. Draw a line to match words that rhyme. The first one is done as an example.

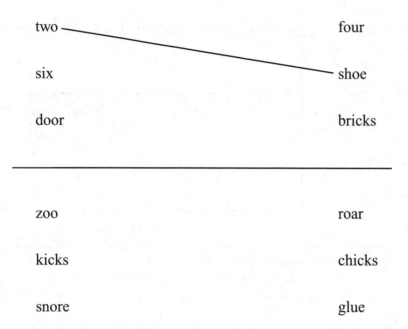

two	four
six	shoe
door	bricks

zoo	roar
kicks	chicks
snore	glue

3. Practice Key Vocabulary words. Write two sentences with two Key Vocabulary words.

   Example: *I have a favorite song.*

   _____

   _____.

   _____

   _____.

ACTIVITY 2: Rhyming

1. Read this nursery rhyme.

   One, Two… Tie My Shoe

   1, 2…

   Tie my shoe.

   3, 4…

   Open the door.

   5, 6…

   Pick up sticks.

   7, 8…

   Lay them straight.

   9, 10…

   A big fat hen.

   > **Rhymes** are words that have the same ending sound.
   >
   > **Examples:**
   >
   > | cat | ten |
   > |-----|-----|
   > | mat | hen |
   > | hat | Ben |
   >
   > Words that rhyme might not be spelled the same.
   >
   > plaque
   >
   > sack

2. Which words rhyme?

   _____

   _____

   _____

   _____

   _____

3. How do you know they rhyme?

   I know they rhyme because _____

   _____ .

3. What words rhyme with *two*? List them.

_____

_____

_____

_____

_____

_____

Rhyming helps children learn about sounds and sound patterns.
Children use what they know about sounds to learn to read.

4. Find and sort rhymes with picture cards.

    ▸ Get picture cards from your teacher.

    ▸ Sort the picture cards that rhyme.

    ▸ Put a picture card in the column that has the same rhyme.

Example: *Put the picture card with the* <u>shoe</u> *in the* **<u>two</u>** *column because* **shoe** *and* **two** *rhyme.*

Rhyming Words
Sorting Chart

Words That Rhyme With "Two"	Words That Rhyme With "Four"	Words That Rhyme With "Six"
Example:		

5. Find and sort rhymes with picture cards.

  ▶ Get picture cards from your teacher.

  ▶ Sort the picture cards that rhyme.

  ▶ Put a picture card in the column that has the same rhyme.

Rhyming Words
Sorting Chart

Words That Rhyme With "Eight"	Words That Rhyme With "Ten"

ACTIVITY 3: Beginning Sounds

1. Listen while your teacher reads a poem.

2. What words begin with the same first sound as *tape*?

_____

_____

_____

_____

_____

> The **beginning sound** is the first sound you hear in a word.

Teresa, the Marquesa

Teresa, the marquesa,
tippi, tippi, tesa,
walks with a jingle,
tippi, tippi, tingle,
bells on her crown,
tippi, tippi, town.

Teresa, la marquesa

Teresa, la marquesa,
tipití, tipitesa,
tenía una corona,
tipití, tipitona,
con cuatro campanillas,
tipití, tipitillas.

¡Pio Peep! Traditional Spanish Nursery Rhymes by Alma Flor Ada & F. Isabel Campoy. Spanish compilation copyright © 2003 by Alma Flor Ada and F. Isabel Campoy. English adaptations copyright © 2003 by Alice Schertle. Illustrations copyright © 2003 by Viví Escrivá. Used by permission of HarperCollins Publishers.

3. What other words begin with the same beginning sound as *tape*? Use English or your home language or both.

_____

_____

_____

_____

_____

ACTIVITY 4: Language Play

1. Listen while your teacher reads this nursery rhyme. Listen for rhyming words.

<table>
<tr><td>

Wide–Awake Chicks

Little baby chicks say
Peep! Peep! Peep!
We're hungry! We're cold!
We won't go to sleep!

Mother hen scratches
for barley and seed
and gives them the warmth
a little chick needs.

Under her wings,
cozy and warm,
little baby chicks
sleep until dawn.

</td><td>

Los Pollitos

Los pollitos dicen:
"pío, pío, pío"
cuando tienen hambre,
cuando tienen frío.

La gallina busca
el maíz y el trigo,
les da la comida
y les presta abrigo.

Bajo sus dos alas
acurrucaditos,
hasta el otro día
duermen los pollitos.

</td></tr>
</table>

¡Pio Peep! Traditional Spanish Nursery Rhymes by Alma Flor Ada & F. Isabel Campoy. Spanish compilation copyright © 2003 by Alma Flor Ada and F. Isabel Campoy. English adaptations copyright © 2003 by Alice Schertle. Illustrations copyright © 2003 by Viví Escrivá. Used by permission of HarperCollins Publishers.

2. Listen for the beginning sound in _peep_ and _pio_. What is it?

3. Play with language. Substitute the beginning sound in _peep_ and _pio_ with /m/. What words do you make?

4. Play with language. Substitute the beginning sound in _peep_ and _pio_ with /l/. What words do you make?

5. What words rhyme with _pio_?

_____

_____

_____

ACTIVITY 5: Think About Today's Lesson

1. Reflect on what you learned. Finish the sentences.

    Today I learned _____

    _____

    _____

    _____ .

    I plan to _____

    _____

    _____

    _____ .

    A question I still have is _____

    _____

    _____

    _____ .

2. Reflect on some important words and ideas you heard in this lesson.

    ▶ Read the words below.

    ▶ With the class, talk about these words.

    ▶ Add any new words you want to remember below.

• rhymes
• sort
• substitute
•
•
•

3. Review the ideas in the lesson.

   Lesson 1: Songs and Nursery Rhymes
   You can help your child learn sounds and sound patterns by singing songs and saying nursery rhymes. Your child can learn about sounds by doing rhyming activities and playing with language. When your child learns about language sounds, it helps him or her learn to read. Your child can learn about sounds in his or her home language or in English.

4. Do you have any other important ideas you learned from this lesson?

   ▶ List them below.

   ▶ Share your ideas with the class.

   _____

   _____

   _____

   _____

Take–Home Activity

LESSON 1: Songs and Nursery Rhymes

Goal
Practice what you learned about rhymes and beginning sounds in class with your child at home.

Objectives
▶ Teach a song or rhyme to your child.

▶ Practice listening for rhyming words in a song or rhyme with your child.

▶ Think of rhyming words with your child.

▶ Practice listening for beginning sounds in words in a song or rhyme with your child.

▶ Substitute beginning letters in words and have fun making new words with your child.

Directions
1. Prepare. Think about the following questions.

   ▶ What song or rhyme do you want to teach your child?

   ▶ What are the rhyming words?

   ▶ What beginning letter will you use to sort words?

2. Try this at home.

   ▶ Teach your child a song or rhyme or ask him or her to teach one to you.

   ▶ Help your child listen for and say the rhyming words in a song or poem.

   ▶ Help your child listen for the beginning sounds in words in a song or poem.

   ▶ Have fun with your child substituting beginning letters in words—make up nonsense words.

   ▶ Do a sorting activity with your child.

3. Review.

▶ Think about what you did with your child. How did it help your child learn language or build reading skills?

▶ Write a sentence about the activity you did with your child. Use the examples if you need help.

_____

_____ .

> **Examples:**
> I sang "Good Morning" with my child.
> My child said a nursery rhyme.
> We did the sorting activity.

4. Reflect.

▶ What did you and your child have fun doing?

We had fun _____

_____ .

▶ What do you think your child learned?

My child learned _____

_____ .

▶ What went well?

_____

_____ went well.

▶ What could go better next time?

_____

_____ could go better next time.

5. Prepare for next class.

▶ Collect songs and nursery rhymes from your home country or childhood.

▶ Bring them to the next class.

Actividad para realizar en el hogar

Lección 1: Cantos y rimas infantiles

Meta

Practicar en casa con su niño lo que ha aprendido acerca de cómo reconocer las rimas y los primeros sonidos.

Objetivos

▶ Enseñarle una canción o rima a su niño.

▶ Practicar con su niño escuchando palabras que riman en una canción o en una rima.

▶ Pensar juntos en palabras que riman.

▶ Practicar escuchando los sonidos iniciales de las palabras en una canción o en una rima.

▶ Sustituir las primeras letras de las palabras y divertirse construyendo nuevas palabras con su niño.

Instrucciones

1. Prepárese. Piense en las siguientes preguntas.

   ▶ ¿Hay alguna canción o rima que desee enseñarle al niño?

   ▶ ¿Puede escoger las palabras que riman?

   ▶ ¿Qué letra inicial usará para clasificar las palabras?

2. Para hacer en casa.

   ▶ Enséñele a su niño una canción o rima o pídale a él o ella que le enseñe una a usted.

   ▶ Ayúdele al niño a escuchar y decir las palabras que riman en la canción o poema.

   ▶ Ayude al niño a escuchar los sonidos iniciales en las palabras de la canción o poema.

   ▶ Diviértase con su niño cambiando las primeras letras de las palabras, y creando así palabras nuevas y a veces palabras sin sentido.

   ▶ Realice una actividad de ordenamiento o clasificación con su niño.

3. Repase.

▶ Piense sobre lo que hizo con su niño. ¿Cómo le ayudó a su niño a aprender habilidades lingüísticas o de lectura?

▶ Escriba una oración sobre la actividad que realizó con el niño. Utilice ejemplos si necesita ayuda.

_____

_____.

> **Ejemplos:**
> Canté "Buenos días" con mi niño.
> Leyó mi niño una rima infantil.
> Hicimos la actividad para clasificar.

4. Reflexione.

▶ ¿Con qué actividad se divirtieron más usted y su niño?

Nos divertimos _____

_____.

▶ ¿Qué cree que aprendió su niño?

Mi niño aprendió _____

_____.

▶ ¿Qué cosas resultaron bien?

_____

_____ resultaron bien.

▶ ¿Qué podría resultar mejor la próxima vez?

_____

_____ podría resultar mejor la próxima vez.

5. Prepárese para la próxima clase.

▶ Junte ejemplos de cantos y rimas infantiles de su país natal o de su infancia.

▶ Tráigalos para la próxima clase.

LESSON 2: Clapping Games and Language Play

Lesson Goal

Practice ways to help your child learn about sounds with clapping games and language play.

Lesson Objectives

Today we will:

▶ Identify the number of syllables in words.

▶ Practice clapping syllables in words.

▶ Share a favorite song or nursery rhyme with the class.

▶ Compile a book of nursery rhymes.

Lesson Warm–Up

1. Share your song or nursery rhyme with the class.

   ▶ When did you learn it?

   ▶ Who taught it to you?

2. Practice poems and nursery rhymes.

   ▶ Sing the *Good Morning/Buenos Dias* song with the class.

   ▶ Say the *Teresa, the Marquesa/Teresa, la marquesa* poem with the class.

3. Read this syllable definition.

   > **Syllables** are units of spoken language that contain one or more vowels.

4. Read this vowel definition.

   > **Vowels** are the *a, e, i, o, u* letters in the English alphabet.

Points to Remember

Play with sounds through activities like clapping syllables and singing songs and nursery rhymes with your child. It will help your child:

▶ Identify sounds in a language.

▶ Identify syllables in a language.

▶ Develop reading skills.

▶ Have fun with language in English or your home language.

Can you add some more important points to this list?

_____

_____

_____

_____

ACTIVITY 1: Key Vocabulary

Words in this lesson are listed below. Use the Key Vocabulary pages to build your vocabulary.

1. Review the words. Which ones do you know?

Word Part	Word	Example	Translation
noun	daddy		
noun	mommy		
noun	poem		
noun	tortillas		
noun	tummy		
noun	vowels		
adjective	hot		
adjective	hungry		
adjective	round		
adjective	yummy		
adverb	nicely		
verb	clap		

2. Practice Key Vocabulary words. Say the nursery rhyme and clap each syllable.

<u>*Tortillas for Mommy*</u>	<u>*Tortillitas para mamá*</u>
Mommy likes tortillas	*Tortillitas para mamá*
Steaming hot and yummy.	*tortillitas para papá.*
Make them round and nicely browned	*Las calentitas para mamá*
For Daddy's hungry tummy.	*Las doraditas para papá.*

¡Pio Peep! Traditional Spanish Nursery Rhymes by Alma Flor Ada & F. Isabel Campoy. Spanish compilation copyright © 2003 by Alma Flor Ada and F. Isabel Campoy. English adaptations copyright © 2003 by Alice Schertle. Illustrations copyright © 2003 by Viví Escrivá. Used by permission of HarperCollins Publishers.

3. Practice Key Vocabulary words. Write the number of syllables on the line next to the word:

<u>*Tortillas for Mommy*</u>

Mommy	_____
likes	_____
tortillas	_____
steaming	_____
hot	_____
and	_____
yummy	_____
make	_____
them	_____
round	_____
nicely	_____
browned	_____
for	_____
Daddy's	_____
hungry	_____
tummy	_____

<u>*Tortillitas para mamá*</u>

tortillitas	_____
para	_____
mamá	_____
papá	_____
las	_____
calentitas	_____
doraditas	_____

4. Practice Key Vocabulary words. Write two sentences with two Key Vocabulary words.

   Example: *My tummy wants food.*

   _____

   _____.

   _____

   _____.

ACTIVITY 2: Clapping Games

1. Say the poem with the class.

    ▶ Listen for the syllables.

    ▶ Clap your hands together for each syllable in a word.

    Teresa, the Marquesa

    Teresa, the marquesa,
    tippi, tippi, tesa,
    walks with a jingle,
    tippi, tippi, tingle,
    bells on her crown,
    tippi, tippi, town.

    ¡Pio Peep! Traditional Spanish Nursery Rhymes by Alma Flor Ada & F. Isabel Campoy.
    Spanish compilation copyright © 2003 by Alma Flor Ada and F. Isabel Campoy. English
    adaptations copyright © 2003 by Alice Schertle. Illustrations copyright © 2003 by Viví
    Escrivá. Used by permission of HarperCollins Publishers.

2. Say the nursery rhyme with the class.

    ▶ Listen for the syllables.

    ▶ Clap your hands together for each syllable in a word.

Tortillas for Mommy	*Tortillitas para mamá*
Mommy likes tortillas	*Tortillitas para mamá*
Steaming hot and yummy.	*tortillitas para papá.*
Make them round and nicely browned	*Las calentitas para mamá*
For Daddy's hungry tummy.	*Las doraditas para papá.*

    ¡Pio Peep! Traditional Spanish Nursery Rhymes by Alma Flor Ada & F. Isabel Campoy.
    Spanish compilation copyright © 2003 by Alma Flor Ada and F. Isabel Campoy. English
    adaptations copyright © 2003 by Alice Schertle. Illustrations copyright © 2003 by Viví
    Escrivá. Used by permission of HarperCollins Publishers.

3. What clapping games do you do with your child?

    _____

    _____

    _____

ACTIVITY 3: Sharing and Teaching Nursery Rhymes from Home

1. Write your poem or nursery rhyme.

Something to Share

Title: _____

Written by: _____

Words:

_____

_____

_____

_____

_____

_____

_____

_____

Picture:

2. Share your song, poem or nursery rhyme you brought from home with your group.

3. Teach your group's song, poem or nursery rhyme to the class.

 ▶ Say the song or nursery rhyme for the class.

 ▶ Give a copy of the song, poem or nursery rhyme to each person in the class.

 ▶ Practice it together with the class.

 ▶ Clap the syllables as you share your song or nursery rhyme.

4. Listen while your classmates teach you a song or nursery rhyme. Pay close attention—it may be in a language that is new to you!

Activity 4: Think About Today's Lesson

1. Reflect on what you learned. Finish the sentences.

Today I learned _____

_____

_____

_____

I plan to _____

_____

_____

_____

A question I still have is _____

_____

_____

_____

2. Reflect on some important ideas and vocabulary words you heard in the lesson.
   ▸ Read the words below.
   ▸ With the class, talk about these words.
   ▸ Add any new words you want to remember below.

   - syllable
   - vowels
   -
   -
   -
   -

3. Review the ideas in the lesson.

Lesson 2: Clapping Games and Language Play
Today we talked about some ways you can help your child become a better reader. When you sing songs, say nursery rhymes and play clapping games with your child, you help your child learn sounds and sound patterns. Sounds and sound patterns help your child connect sounds to letters when he or she reads. Your child can learn about sounds in your home language, in English or in both.

4. Do you have any other important ideas you learned from this lesson?
   ▶ List them below.
   ▶ Share your ideas with the class.

_____

_____

_____

_____

Take–Home Activity

LESSON 2: Clapping Games and Language Play

Goal

Share what you learned in class about playing with language through clapping activities and reading poems, nursery rhymes and songs with your child.

Objectives

▶ Identify the number of syllables in words with your child.

▶ Practice clapping word syllables with your child.

▶ Teach a song or nursery rhyme to your child.

▶ Share your book of nursery rhymes and songs from class with your child.

Directions

1. Prepare. Think about the following questions.

   ▶ How did your teacher show you how to clap syllables?

   ▶ Which song or nursery rhyme will you teach your child?

   ▶ How does clapping syllables and saying nursery rhymes help your child develop language skills?

2. Try this at home.

   ▶ Share the book of nursery rhymes and songs that you made in class.

   ▶ Teach a rhyme, poem or song to your child.

   ▶ Help your child identify syllables in words.

   ▶ Practice clapping word syllables with your child.

   ▶ Ask your child to teach you a nursery rhyme he or she knows.

3. Review.
   After you spend time with your child, think about the following questions. Write your thoughts and answers in the space below. We will discuss them in our next class.

   ▶ What did you read with your child?

   We read _____

   _____.

▶ What did you use to clap syllables?

We clapped syllables to _____

_____.

▶ What did you sing with your child?

We sang _____

_____.

4. Reflect.

▶ What did you and your child have fun doing?

We had fun _____

_____.

▶ What do you think your child learned?

My child learned _____

_____.

▶ What went well?

_____

_____ went well.

▶ What could go better next time?

_____

_____ could go better next time.

Actividad para realizar en el hogar

LECCIÓN 2: Juegos con aplauso y juegos con el lenguaje

Meta

Compartir con su niño lo que aprendió en la clase sobre cómo puede jugar con el lenguaje a través de actividades para aplaudir y a través de la lectura de cantos y rimas infantiles.

Objetivos:

▶ Identificar con su niño el número de sílabas que tienen las palabras.

▶ Practicar aplaudiendo con su niño en cada sílaba.

▶ Enseñarle a su niño un canto o rimas infantiles.

▶ Compartir con su niño su libro de rimas y canciones infantiles que obtuvo en la clase.

Instrucciones

1. Prepárese. Piense en las siguientes preguntas.

   ▶ ¿Cómo le mostró su maestro a aplaudir en cada sílaba?

   ▶ ¿Qué canto o rima infantil le va a enseñar a su niño?

   ▶ ¿Cómo puede ayudarle a su niño el aplaudir en las sílabas y el recitar rimas a desarrollar habilidades lingüísticas?

2. Para hacer en casa.

   ▶ Comparta el libro de cantos y rimas infantiles que hizo en clase.

   ▶ Enséñele a su niño una rima, poema o una canción.

   ▶ Ayúdelo a identificar las sílabas en las palabras.

   ▶ Practique con el niño, aplaudiendo en las sílabas de las palabras.

   ▶ Pídale al niño que le enseñe una rima infantil que conozca.

3. Repase.
   Después de que pase tiempo con su niño, piense en las siguientes preguntas. Escriba sus ideas y respuestas en el espacio que tiene a continuación. En nuestra próxima clase hablaremos sobre ellas.

   ▶ ¿Qué leyó con su niño?

   Leímos _____

   _____.

▶ ¿Qué usaron para aplaudir las sílabas?

Aplaudimos _____

_____ .

▶ ¿Qué cantó con su niño?

Cantamos _____

_____ .

4. Reflexione.

▶ ¿Con qué actividad se divirtieron más usted y su niño?

Nos divertimos _____

_____ .

▶ ¿Qué cree que aprendió su niño?

Mi niño aprendió _____

_____ .

▶ ¿Qué cosas resultaron bien?

_____

_____ resultaron bien.

▶ ¿Qué podría resultar mejor la próxima vez?

_____

_____ podría resultar mejor la próxima vez.

This survey is to evaluate the unit on **Playing With Language**. There are no wrong answers and you will not be asked to talk about your answers.

1. What information did you learn from the Playing With Language unit?

    _____

    _____

    _____

2. What else would you like to know about the Playing With Language unit?

    _____

    _____

    _____

3. How will the information help you help your child?

    _____

    _____

    _____

4. Check (✔) one of the following statements about this unit.

    _____ I understood everything.

    _____ I understood most of it.

    _____ I understood some of it.

    _____ I understood a little of it.

    _____ I did not understand any of it.

    When you have finished this survey, please give it to your teacher.

Esta encuesta es para evaluar la unidad de **Juegos con el lenguaje**. No existen respuestas incorrectas y no se le pedirá que comente lo que respondió.

1. ¿Qué cosas aprendió en la unidad de Juegos con el lenguaje?

_____

_____

_____

2. ¿Qué otras cosas le gustarían saber acerca de la unidad de Juegos con el lenguaje?

_____

_____

_____

3. ¿De qué manera le ayudará a usted esta información para poder ayudar a su niño?

_____

_____

_____

4. Marque (✔) sólo una de las siguientes afirmaciones sobre esta unidad.

_____ Entendí todo.

_____ Entendí la mayoría de las cosas.

_____ Entendí algunas cosas.

_____ Entendí un poco.

_____ No entendí en absoluto.

Cuando haya finalizado esta encuesta, entréguesela a su maestro.